CAROLS FOR CHOIR AND CONGREGATION

By Joseph M. Martin
Orchestration by Brant Adams

CONT

Free, reproducible congregation parts are available at www.shawneepress.com in the "Closer Look" feature of item 35028883.

Harold Flammer
MUSIC

A DIVISION OF SHAWNEE PRESS, INC.
EXCLUSIVELY DISTRIBUTED BY HAL LEONARD CORPORATION

Visit Shawnee Press Online at
www.shawneepress.com

FOREWORD

Each season, at the approach of Advent and Christmas, there arises in the church a renewed energy for singing and musical expression. Deeply imbedded in the heart of the worshipping church are the great carols, both new and ancient, that animate the spirit and invigorate the heart. The echoes of these great monuments of praise ring strong in the halls of our sanctuaries. When we lift them up in praise, we are connected with a community of song that goes back centuries. They are a treasured part of our seasonal celebrations and an essential element in our language of worship.

This present volume of "Christmas Classics" provides for an illuminated congregational singing experience by decorating these time-honored carols with colorful orchestrations and supportive choral parts. These arrangements seek to invigorate and support congregational participation and provide memorable moments for all of those gathered to celebrate in song our common faith.

Let there be music!

JOSEPH M. MARTIN

Free, reproducible congregation parts are available at www.shawneepress.com in the "Closer Look" feature of item 35028883.

O COME, ALL YE FAITHFUL

for S.A.T.B. voices and congregation, accompanied

Words
Latin Hymn
Attributed to
JOHN FRANCIS WADE (1711-1786)

Tune: **ADESTE FIDELES**
by JOHN FRANCIS WADE (1711-1786)
Arranged by
JOSEPH M. MARTIN (BMI)

CHOIR *and* CONGREGATION

come, let us a-dore Him. O come, let us a-dore Him. O

come, let us a-dore___ Him,___ Christ_____ the Lord!

Lord!

cresc. poco a poco

allargando

SOPRANO DESCANT
with triumph

f

Yea,   Lord,   we greet   Thee,   born   this

S. **f** *unis.*

A.

Yea,   Lord,   we greet   Thee,   born this hap - py

T. **f** *unis.*

B.

with triumph

f

COME, THOU LONG-EXPECTED JESUS

for S.A.T.B. voices and congregation, accompanied

Words by
CHARLES WESLEY (1707-1788)

Based on tune: **HYFRYDOL**
by ROWLAND H. PRICHARD (1811-1887)
Arranged by
JOSEPH M. MARTIN (BMI)

long - ex - pect - ed Je - sus, born___ to___ set Thy___

peo - ple free. From___ our fears___ and sins___ re -

lease___ us; let___ us find our___ rest___ in Thee.

joy_____ of ev - 'ry long - ing heart.

Born Thy peo - ple to de - liv - er,

born a child, and yet,___ a king, born to reign___ in us for - ev - er, now Thy gra - cious king - dom bring.

66

By Thine all_____ suf - fi - cient mer - it,

70

raise us to_____ Thy glo - rious throne!

74

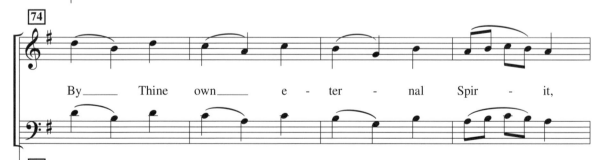

By_____ Thine own_____ e - ter - nal Spir - it,

rule in all_____ our hearts a - lone.

CHOIR *only*

Come, O

Come,___ Em - man - u - el!_____

O COME, O COME, EMMANUEL

for S.A.T.B. voices and congregation, accompanied

Words: Latin hymn
Translation by
JOHN MASON NEALE (1818-1866)
and HENRY SLOANE COFFIN (1877-1954)

Based on tune:
VENI EMMANUEL
15th Century Plainsong
Arranged by
JOSEPH M. MARTIN (BMI)

Lyrics:
(*f*) come, O come, Em - man - u - el, and ran - som cap - tive
(*mf*) come, Thou Day - spring, come and cheer our spir - its by Thine

O

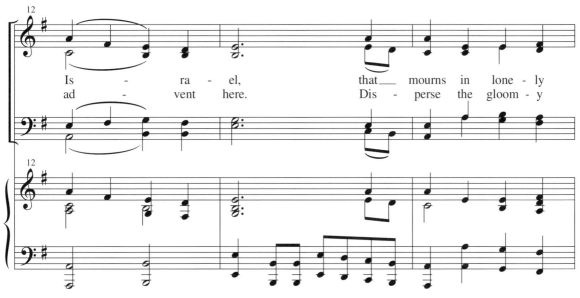

Is - ra - el, that__ mourns in lone - ly
ad - vent here. Dis - perse the gloom - y

ex - ile here, un - til the Son of
clouds_____ of night, and death's dark shad - ows

God_____ ap - pear. Re - joice! Re -
put_____ to flight.

20

joice! Em - man - u - el shall

come to thee, O Is - ra - el. O el.

el shall come to thee, O Is - ra -

el! Come, O___ come Em - man - u -

CHOIR *only*

el.

dedicated to my mother-in-law, Cleva Collar, and her family
in celebration of the life of Robert Jay Collar who loved to sing

O HOLY NIGHT

for S.A.T.B. voices and congregation, accompanied

Words by
JOHN S. DWIGHT (1813-1893)

Tune: **CANTIQUE DE NOËL**
by ALDOLPHE ADAM (1803-1856)
Arranged by
JOSEPH M. MARTIN (BMI)

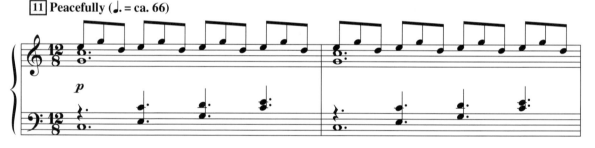

CHOIR *and* CONGREGATION
SOPRANO *and* ALTO *or* SOLO

O   ho - ly night,_____ the   stars   are   bright - ly

shin - ing. It is the night of the dear Sav - ior's

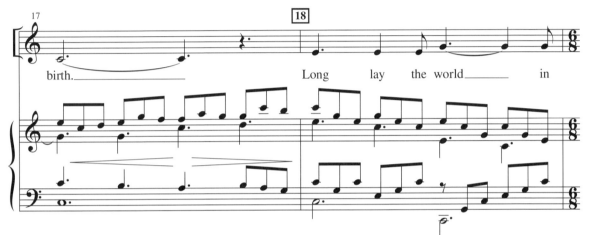

birth._____ Long lay the world_____ in

sin and er - ror pin - ing, till He ap -

peared and the soul felt its worth._____ A

thrill of hope, the wea - ry world re - joic - es, for

(opt. solo ends)

yon - der breaks a new and glo - rious morn.

Fall_____ on your knees. O

love one an - oth - er. His law is

love and His gos - pel is peace.

God is our friend, for Christ is now our

broth - er, and in His name all op - pres - sion shall

cease. Sweet hymns of joy in

grate - ful cho - rus raise we. Let all with - in us

55 CHOIR and CONGREGATION
54
f
praise His ho - ly name. Christ is the
Lord! O praise His name for -
ev - er. O night di -
56
58

O LITTLE TOWN OF BETHLEHEM

for S.A.T.B. voices and congregation, accompanied

Words by
PHILLIPS BROOKS (1835-1893)

Tune: **ST. LOUIS**
by LEWIS H. REDNER (1831-1908)
Arranged by
JOSEPH M. MARTIN (BMI)

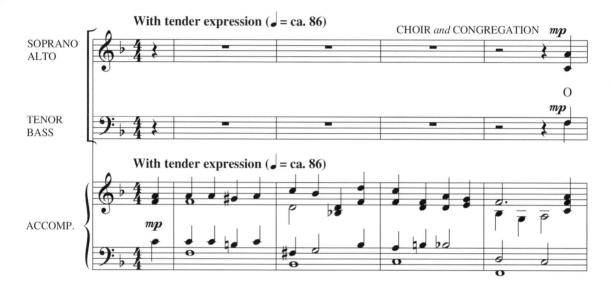

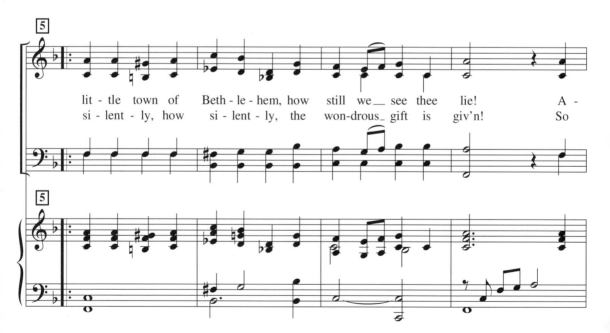

bove thy deep and dream-less sleep the si - lent stars go by. Yet
God im-parts to hu - man hearts the bless-ings of His heav'n. No

in thy dark streets shin - eth the ev - er - last - ing light. The
ear may hear His com - ing, but in this world of sin, where

hopes and fears of all the years are met in thee to - night. How
meek souls will re - ceive Him, still the dear Christ en - ters

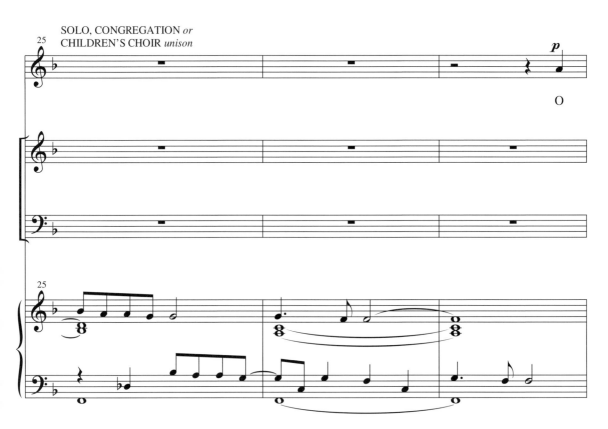

28 *a tempo*

ho - ly Child of Beth - le - hem, de - scend to __ us, we pray. Cast

(Accompanist may double voices if desired.)

a tempo

S. **pp**

A.

Oo _____

T. **pp**

B.

32

out our sin, and en - ter in. Be born in __ us to - day! We

mp

We

36

hear the Christ - mas an - gels the great glad tid - ings

hear the Christ - mas __ an - gels the great glad tid - ings

mp

tell. O come to us, a - bide with us, our Lord Im - man - u -

tell. O come to us, a - bide with us, our Lord Im - man - u -

CHOIR *only*

el! Our Lord Im - man - u - el!

el! Our Lord Im - man - u - el!

ANGELS WE HAVE HEARD ON HIGH

for S.A.T.B. voices and congregation, accompanied

Words
Traditional French Carol

Tune: **GLORIA**
Traditional French Carol
Arranged by
JOSEPH M. MARTIN (BMI)

With a fanfare of joy (♩ = ca. 108)

12

CHOIR *and* CONGREGATION

An - gels we have heard on high, sweet - ly sing - ing
Shep - herds, why this ju - bi - lee? Why your joy - ous

o'er the plains; and the moun - tains in re - ply,
strains pro - long? What the glad - some tid - ings be

ech - o - ing their joy - ous strains.
which in - spire your heav'n - ly song?

Glo - - -

- ri - a____ in ex - cel - sis De - o!

Glo - - -

42

-ri - a___ in ex - cel - sis De - o!

o!

in ex - cel - sis De - o!

CHOIR *only*

Glo - ri - a in ex-cel - sis De - o!

Glo - ri - a in ex-cel - sis De - o!

Gloria in excelsis Deo!

Gloria! Gloria!

Gloria! Gloria!

Gloria! in excelsis Deo!

CRADLE CAROLS

for S.A.T.B. voices and congregation, accompanied

Tunes:
MUELLER
ST. LOUIS
STILLE NACHT
Arranged by
JOSEPH M. MARTIN (BMI)

Lyrics:

* A - way in a man - ger, no crib for a
near me, Lord Je - sus, I ask Thee to

bed, the lit - tle Lord Je - sus lay down His sweet
stay close by me for - ev - er, and love me, I

* Tune: MUELLER, James R. Murray, 1841-1905
Words: St. 1, anonymous; st. 2, John Thomas McFarland, 1851-1913

head. The stars in the bright sky looked down where He
pray. Bless all the dear chil - dren in Thy ten - der

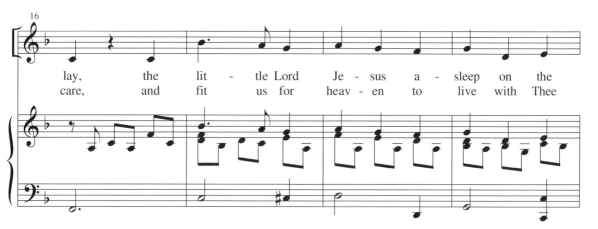

lay, the lit - tle Lord Je - sus a - sleep on the
care, and fit us for heav - en to live with Thee

hay. Be there.

50

* Tune: ST. LOUIS, Lewis H. Redner, 1831-1908
  Words: Phillips Brooks, 1835-1893

CAROLS FOR CHOIR AND CONGREGATION - SATB

light; the hopes and fears of all the years are__ met in__ thee to-
night.

CHOIR *and* CONGREGATION

46 **Peacefully (♩ = ca. 80)**

* *p* Si - lent night,
mp Si - lent night,

ho - ly night! All is calm, all is
ho - ly night! Shep - herds quake at the

* Tune: STILLE NACHT, Franz Gruber, 1787-1863
  Words: Joseph Mohr, 1792-1848; tr. John Freeman Young, 1820-1885, and anonymous, st. 2

A CHRISTMAS TRILOGY

for S.A.T.B. voices and congregation, accompanied

Tunes:
ANTIOCH
THE FIRST NOEL
MENDELSSOHN
Arranged by
JOSEPH M. MARTIN (BMI)

Quickly, with great celebration (♩ = ca. 86)

ACCOMP.

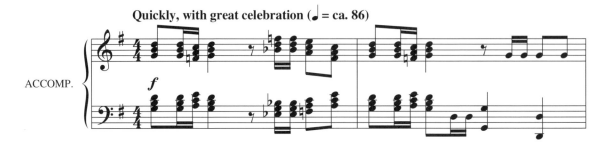

* Tune: ANTIOCH, George Frederick Handel, 1685-1759
Words: Isaac Watts, 1674-1748

CAROLS FOR CHOIR AND CONGREGATION - SATB

heav'n,___ and heav'n_____ and na - ture sing.

heav'n,___ and heav'n and na - ture sing.

CHOIR *only*

S. **mf** *unis.*

A.

Joy to the earth! the Sav - ior reigns. Let

T.

B.

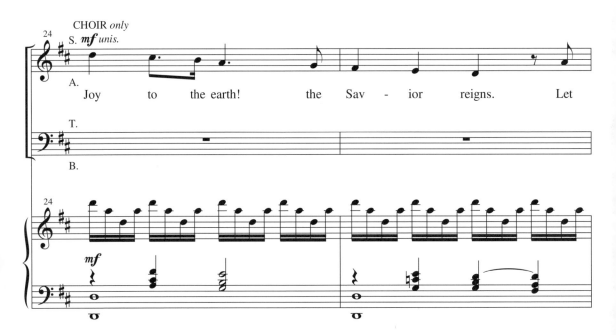

sound - ing joy!   * The__

first_____ No - el_____ the__ an - gel did__ say, was to

cer - tain poor shep - herds in fields__ as they lay; in__

A little faster, with festive energy (♩ = ca. 97)

CHOIR *and* **CONGREGATION**

*Hark! the her-ald an-gels sing,___ "Glo-ry to the new-born King.

* Tune: MENDELSSOHN, Felix Mendelssohn, 1809-1847
Words: Charles Wesley, 1707-1788

CAROLS FOR CHOIR AND CONGREGATION - SATB

62

Peace on earth, and mer - cy mild.___ God and sin - ners re - con - ciled!" Joy - ful, all ye na - tions rise.___ Join the tri - umph of the skies.___ With th'an - gel - ic

hosts pro - claim, "Christ is____ born in Beth - le - hem!"

Hark! the her - ald an - gels sing, "Glo - ry____ to the

new - born King."

born to raise the sons of earth, born to give them
(us all from) *(us)*

born to raise the sons of earth, born to__ give them
(us all from) *(us)*

sec - ond birth. Hark! the her - ald an - gels sing,

sec - ond birth. Hark! the her - ald an - gels sing,

119
cresc.
"Glo - ry to the new - born
cresc.
"Glo - ry to the new - born
cresc.
119
cresc.
121
ff
King."
ff
King."
ff
121
ff

SILENT NIGHT, HOLY NIGHT

for S.A.T.B. voices and congregation, accompanied

Words by
JOSEPH MOHR (1792-1848)
Translation by
JOHN FREEMAN YOUNG (1820-1885)
and anonymous, St. 2

Tune: **STILLE NACHT**
by FRANZ GRUBER (1787-1863)
Arranged by
JOSEPH M. MARTIN (BMI)

* Accompaniment is optional through measure 27.

70

72

Christ,___ the Sav - ior, is born!"

Si - lent night, ho - ly night!

CHOIR *only*
mf unis.

Son of God, love's pure light_____ ra - diant beams_____ from Thy ho - ly face, with the dawn of re - deem - ing

74